POW POW POW POW POW POW POW POW POW BIG GUNS

Written by Nina Segal

21 March – 8 April 2017
The Yard Theatre

T0347905

LOTTERY FUNDED | ARTS COUNCIL ENGLAND
Supported using public funding by

Cast
In alphabetical order
Two   Debra Baker
One   Jessye Romeo

Creative Team
Director   Dan Hutton
Designer   Rosie Elnile
Lighting Designer   Katharine Williams
Sound Designer   Kieran Lucas
Production Manager   Ben Karakashian
Stage Manager   Roisin Symes
Publicity Design   Pentagram Design

Big Guns was originally produced at The Yard Theatre in association with Martha Rose Wilson.

The original production was supported by Arts Council England.

Debra Baker

Theatre work includes: *Carry On Jaywick* (UK Tour/The Vaults London); *Wretch* (The Vaults, London); Philip Ridley's plays *Radiant Vermin* (Tobacco Factory Theatres/Soho Theatre/59E59 Theaters), *Mercury Fur* (Theatre Delicatessen), and *Vincent River* (Old Red Lion). Other theatre includes: *Home Theatre* (Theatre Royal Stratford East); *Unexpected Item* (Barbican); *Someone to Blame* (King's Head). Film work includes the recent hit cinema adaptation of the National Theatre's verbatim musical *London Road*.

Debra has appeared in over 20 BBC Radio 4 dramas and was a member of the BBC Radio Drama Company in 2015. Her TV credits include Stephen Poliakoff's *Close To The Enemy* (BBC One), *Birds of a Feather* (ITV), *Phoneshop* (Channel 4) and *Call the Midwife* (BBC One).

Jessye Romeo

Theatre work includes *Dogs Don't Last Forever* (Itch & Scratch); *Martyr* (Unicorn Theatre); *If Chloe Can* (NYT); *Our Days Of Rage* (NYT).

Television includes *Will* (TNT) and *Dirty, Sexy, Things* (Betty TV/Channel 4, Various). Film includes *Mindhorn* (Scott Free Productions & BBC Films) and *The Somnambulists* (No Bad Films).

Nina Segal

Nina Segal is a playwright based in London and New York. Her debut play *In The Night Time (Before The Sun Rises)* premiered at the Gate Theatre in 2016. Upcoming works include: *Becky and Lucy* (New Ohio, NY, 2017/18); and *That Something Exists* (Bushwick Starr Reading Series, 2017; in development with HOME and HighTide). Nina has been a finalist for the Yale Drama Series Prize 2016 and the Adrian Pagan Award 2015 and is currently under commission with HighTide.

Dan Hutton

Directing credits include: *Garden* (How Small How Far, touring); *Still.Waiting* (St James RE:act); *The Spanish Tragedy* (Old Red Lion); *Attempts on Her Life* (Warwick Arts Centre); *Fascism Anyone?* (IATL, Warwick). Assistant Directing includes: *The Glass Menagerie* (Headlong, touring); *Pioneer* (curious directive, touring); *Cat On A Hot Tin Roof* (Royal & Derngate, Northern Stage & Royal Exchange). Dan is a founding member of Barrel Organ.

Rosie Elnile

Rosie studied Design for The Stage at the Royal Central School of Speech and Drama. She was first Resident Design Assistant at The Donmar Warehouse 2015-2016.

Selected credits include: *The Convert* (Gate Theatre); *Macbeth* (Mountview Academy of Theatre); *Hard C*ck* (Spill Festival); *The Half Of It* (RADA Festival); *Loaded* (Jacksons Lane Theatre).

Work as associate designer includes: *Seventeen* (Lyric Theatre Hammersmith); *Elegy* (Donmar Warehouse).

Katharine Williams

Katharine Williams is a lighting designer for live performance. She works in the UK and internationally and recent designs include: *Two Man Show* and *The Darkest Corners* (RashDash); *Safe House* (Daniel Bye); *Partus* (Third Angel). Katharine is lead artist of the Love Letters to the Home Office project which campaigns using art, words and theatre to stop the means-tested tiering of Human Rights that is currently in place in the UK for international families. She is the founder of the Crew for Calais initiative, which is what happens when people from the theatre and creative industries come together to help refugees.

Kieran Lucas

Kieran is a London based sound designer and theatre-maker, founding member of Barrel Organ and associate artist of Coney. Kieran has worked with various theatre companies and venues including Coney, Filter, John Wright, the Royal Shakespeare Company, the Roundhouse, Camden People's Theatre and Battersea Arts Centre as a sound designer, musician, composer, technician and performer as well as creating and devising his own work. Selected credits include: *Blasted* (Styx); *Grown Up* (CPT); *Under the Skin* (St. Paul's Cathedral); *REMOTE* (CPT); *Spanish Tragedy* (Old Red Lion); *Some People Talk About Violence* (touring); *LARDO* (Old Red Lion); *Lost In Blue* (touring); *NOTHING* (touring).

Ben Karakashian

Ben Karakashian graduated from Royal Holloway University of London with a BA Honors in Drama and Theatre Studies.

Production management credits include *New Nigerians* (Arcola Theatre); *Death Takes a Holiday* (Charing Cross Theatre); *Acedian Pirates* (Theatre 503); *Ragtime* (Charing Cross Theatre); *Frontier Trilogy* (Rabenhof Theatre, Vienna); *Home Chat* (Finborough Theatre); *Titanic the Musical* (Charing Cross Theatre); *Kenny Morgan* (Arcola Theatre); *In the Bar of a Tokyo Hotel* (Charing Cross Theatre); *The Divided Laing* (Arcola Theatre); *The Frontier Trilogy* (Edinburgh Fringe Festival); *Contact.com* (Park Theatre); *The Mikado* (Charing Cross Theatre); *The Man Who Shot Liberty Valance* (Park Theatre); *Our Ajax* (Southwark Playhouse); *The Bunker Trilogy* (Southwark Playhouse, Seoul Performing Arts Festival, Stratford Circus).

Martha Rose Wilson

Martha is a freelance producer. She is producer at The Coterie, which she co-runs with artistic director Caitlin McLeod, supported by The Old Vic, RSC and Sky Arts.

Martha is producer at Metal Rabbit Productions and has produced several world premieres including Philip Ridley's *Tonight with Donny Stixx* (The Bunker Theatre); Philip Ridley's *Radiant Vermin* (Tobacco Factory / Soho Theatre / 59E59 Theaters, New York); Tess Berry-Hart's *Cargo* (Arcola Theatre); Mike Stone's *Lardo* (Old Red Lion Theatre); Andrew Muir's *The Session* (Soho Theatre); Neil Bartlett's adaptation of *A Christmas Carol* (Old Red Lion Theatre); Bradley Rand Smith's adaptation of *Johnny Got His Gun* (UK premiere, Southwark Playhouse / UK tour).

Martha was one of the original Old Vic 12 and produced *Prince of the River* by Sam Bailey, directed by Ed Stambollouian (Criterion Theatre). She was producer at the Old Vic New Voices Festival where she produced *Comment is Free* by Bruntwood winner James Fritz, directed by JMK winner Kate Hewitt and *Sirius* by Steven Hevey, directed by Olivier winner Jessica Swale.

Martha has worked as production assistant on Deirdre Kinahan's *Rise* (The Old Vic) directed by Alexander Ferris, and as assistant producer on Tiny Fires' inaugural production *My Mother Said I Never Should* by Charlotte Keatley (St. James Theatre).

In April 2016 Martha was awarded a Stage One Bursary for New Producers and is mentored by Lilli Geissendorfer, Producer at the Almeida Theatre.

Built in 2011 by Founder and Artistic Director Jay Miller, The Yard is a multi-award-winning theatre and bar based in a converted warehouse in Hackney Wick, overlooking the Queen Elizabeth Olympic Park. The Yard Theatre provides a safe space for artists to grow new ideas, and for audiences to access outstanding new work at affordable prices.

"One of London's most exciting new theatres" **The Guardian**

We actively seek out new theatre makers and new audiences. We nurture new artists and help to discover new talent. We help artists produce new work, by offering a platform that enables theatre makers to take risks.

The Yard Theatre is committed to:
1. Exposing stories from unheard voices.
2. Interrogating the process of writing for performance.
3. Discovering and developing new artists.

In our short existence we have had significant success. This includes transfers to the National Theatre for Beyond Caring and Chewing Gum Dreams, and numerous awards including two Peter Brook Empty Space Awards. Success has also led to partnerships with leading theatres and organisations; recent partners include the Young Vic, Royal Court Theatre, National Theatre and HighTide Festival Theatre.

"The most important theatre in east London" **Time Out**

The Yard Theatre encourages audiences to take risks on new work. We do this by making work about the people in our locale, keeping our ticket prices low and by offering our local community opportunities to be involved in the making process.

Alongside the theatre, we run a programme of events, including music nights which fill our bar and contribute to our unique atmosphere. The Yard Theatre also manages Hub67, a community centre in Hackney Wick – a place for neighbours, young people and creative ideas.

The Yard Theatre brings artists and audiences together in an exciting environment where anything becomes possible.

Recent productions include:

- *Beyond Caring* by Alexander Zeldin, which transferred to the National Theatre and has recently completed a national tour ("quietly devastating" ★★★★ *The Guardian*)

- *The Mikvah Project* written by Josh Azouz, directed by Jay Miller, which played a sold-out, extended run ("Every moment feels rich with meaning" ★★★★ *Time Out*)

- *LINES* written by Pamela Carter, directed by Jay Miller, which received substantial critical acclaim ("directed with finesse by The Yard's properly talented artistic director Jay Miller" ★★★★ *Time Out*)

- *Made Visible* written by Deborah Pearson, which sparked lively debate ("a serious examination of racism and the inadequacies of liberalism" ★★★★ *The Guardian*)

- *Removal Men* written by M. J. Harding, with Jay Miller, which received two Off West End Award nominations ("Jay Miller's mesmerically intense production uses music to carve out a space for huge ideas" ★★★★ Time Out)

Nina Segal

BIG GUNS

OBERON BOOKS
LONDON

WWW.OBERONBOOKS.COM

First published in 2017 by Oberon Books Ltd
521 Caledonian Road, London N7 9RH
Tel: +44 (0) 20 7607 3637 / Fax: +44 (0) 20 7607 3629
e-mail: info@oberonbooks.com
www.oberonbooks.com

A catalogue record for this book is available from the British
Library.

PB ISBN: 9781786821669
E ISBN: 9781786821676

Cover design by Pentagram Design

eBook conversion by CPI Group (UK) Ltd, Croydon, CR0 4YY.

Characters

ONE

TWO

The stage is empty except for two actors and two microphones and a vast array of brightly-coloured plastic guns.

The kind of guns with tactile plastic buttons that go

pow pow pow pow pow
kapow pow pow pow
br-br-br-br-br-br-br-br-br-br-boom
when you press them.

So you like to press them.

The actors speak into the microphones at
the-speed-of-rapid-fire and
ignore the guns.

And maybe there aren't any guns at all, not really.
But their presence –

Their presence is there.

1.

ONE: All the things we are.

TWO: All the things we could have become.

ONE: We need more – time.

TWO: Not more –

Not more –

Just –

ONE: More time.

TWO: Yes, more – time.

ONE: Everything would have been better.

TWO: We would have been better.

ONE: We would have made amends.

TWO: We would have earned forgiveness.

ONE: We would have –

TWO: Started over and –

ONE: We would have been –

TWO: Much better.

ONE: So –

TWO: So –

ONE: Much better.

TWO: If we only had more time.

ONE:	If you've ever been beaten –
TWO:	If you've ever seen beatings –
ONE:	If you've ever seen
	hits or
	kicks or
	punches,
	to the
	face or
	the body or
	the nice white set of teeth –
TWO:	You'll know –
ONE:	There's always a moment.
TWO:	Always a moment,
	just – before.
ONE:	Just long enough to
	notice the 'just – before'.
TWO:	That moment –
ONE:	This moment, when you –
TWO:	He –
ONE:	They –
TWO:	Know.
ONE:	When you say –
TWO:	No.
ONE:	When you say –
TWO:	Please.
ONE:	When you see –
TWO:	Fist or –
ONE:	Bat or –
TWO:	Boot or –
ONE:	Bullet.

TWO:	Hi-tech ray gun or hydrogen bomb.
ONE:	In a darkened alley or on the edge of the horizon –
TWO:	Travelling faster than the twenty-four hour news.
ONE:	It's coming.
TWO:	You know it's coming.
ONE:	And as you gather children close at night and tell them tales of how the good guys never bleed or break –
TWO:	You still know that it's coming.
ONE:	Closer.
TWO:	Closer.
ONE:	Always closer.
TWO:	So close you can taste it, smell it, feel the sweet swell of it.
ONE:	It's not safe, these days, but where is?
TWO:	These days.
ONE:	It's alright to feel scared.
TWO:	It's alright to feel threatened.
ONE:	It's coming but –
TWO:	It's not here yet.
ONE:	It'll be here soon –

TWO:	But not quite yet.
ONE:	Just – before.
TWO:	Just long enough before to still believe the tight-curled fist will always freeze just precious seconds from your fragile face, as the camera pans 360 and on the colour television in the other corner of the room, the white man in the crisp black leather puts his hand out and the bullets just stop and hang there –
ONE:	Motionless.
TWO:	Obedient.
ONE:	In a moment, they'll drop to the ground, won't they?
TWO:	Won't they?
ONE:	They always do.
TWO:	Don't they?

One of the actors carries a large black sack onto the stage.

The sack is heavy and straining and opaque,
full of rubble or kittens or humans or
appropriately separated recyclable materials.

They deposit the black sack and we all look at it with
unequal mix of fear and curiosity,
like a one-night-stand or
an unattended suitcase in
a busy railway station.

Maybe it moves.

Maybe it moves just a little,
in the corner of your eye and
the pitch-black part of your brain.

Or maybe,
like the guns,

there's no black sack at all.

3

ONE: Her name is –
       Em.
       Probably Emily,
       maybe Emma,
       or maybe something else,
       something with more syllables,
       something that makes all the xenophobes tut when
       she spells it out,
       letter-by-letter,
       on the crowded bus in
       the midday traffic.
       But to me,
       to you,
       to all of us,
       to all of us here,
       together –
       Em.

TWO: You know this because it's written in
       the front of the diary.

ONE: Not 'Em's Diary',
       of course not,
       not that juvenile,
       not that feminine,
       not that public a statement.

TWO: Just that single word,
       that single sound –

ONE: 'Em'.

TWO: All caps,
       thick felt tip,
       on the inside front cover,

	beneath a doodle of
	a thick-trunked stunted tree.
ONE:	Fat-ass tree.
TWO:	It doesn't say it,
	but you know it's a diary.
	You know it's a diary because
	after you find it –
ONE:	Jammed down the side of the
	save-for-disabled on the
	North-heading 148 –
TWO:	And after you pick it up –
ONE:	Silently reasoning that it being jammed in there,
	not an accident to leave this left there,
	for someone,
	somebody,
	(not necessarily you but
	certainly not *not* you) –
	to find it.
TWO:	To pick it up.
ONE:	To open it.
TWO:	To look inside.
ONE:	To absent-mindedly form
	your mouth into the
	perfectly circular shape
	of the sound as you read:
TWO:	'Em'.
ONE:	After the finding,
	the happening-across, really,
	the prising out between
	seat pad and
	chewing gum,

	the taking home,
	the opening –
TWO:	The wondering about this
	half-girl-half-tree-fat-ass-anonymous-author –
ONE:	The mouthing of the word –
TWO:	'Em'.
ONE:	After all that,
	finally –
	the reading.
TWO:	Bullet-point descriptions of
	physical flaws and
	philosophical misgivings.
ONE:	Elongated love letters full of
	metaphors that fall
	just the wrong side of romantic.
TWO:	Long entries identified not by
	date or location but by
	red pen lists of foods consumed and
	real-time self-loathing levels.
ONE:	And the entry under
	'Mac and cheese,
	green salad,
	chocolate fucking raisins,
	sad face' reads:
TWO:	'It's scary, really.'
ONE:	'It's actually really scary.'
TWO:	'How easy it is?'
ONE:	'How close it is?'
TWO:	'You think it's far away, or – '
ONE:	'You think you're far away from it.'
TWO:	'But really.'

ONE:	'It just takes one – '
TWO:	'Mistake.'
ONE:	'One – '
TWO:	'Wrong turn.'
ONE:	'One – '
TWO:	'Moment, tiny moment, tiny useless moment just – before.'
ONE:	'One false move and it all falls down.'
TWO:	'Makes me feel – sick.'
ONE:	'When I think about it.'
TWO:	'How close it is and what "it" is.'
ONE:	'What. "It." Is.'
TWO:	And then a deep black scribbled-over hole, the paper ripped by the force of the redaction.
ONE:	And then, a list:
TWO:	'Tsunamis.'
ONE:	'Financial collapse.'
TWO:	'Missing children.'
ONE:	'Missing fingers.'
TWO:	'Men with vans with doors that lock from the outside.'

ONE:	'Train crash.'
TWO:	'Back fat.'
ONE:	'Structural weakness.'
TWO:	'Social disease.'
ONE:	'Human error' and
	also further down,
	just 'HUMAN',
	in all caps and
	all alone.
TWO:	'The feeling that we're just – '
ONE:	'Before.'
TWO:	'Something.'
ONE:	'Something.'
BOTH:	'Soon.'
TWO:	And after you've devoured every single word,
	every fault and fear,
	missed meal and
	missed opportunity,
	more than once if truth be told,
	and realised that what you are reading is,
	in fact,
	a diary –
ONE:	You've already crossed a line.
TWO:	You've already gone too far.
ONE:	You don't read people's diaries.
TWO:	People don't read other people's diaries.
ONE:	Of course, sometimes it
	does happen.
TWO:	Unintentionally, of course,
	really just an instinct of
	your eyes and

	your brain and
	your fingers,
	to read –
ONE:	'Burning buildings.'
TWO:	To take in –
ONE:	'Birth defects.'
TWO:	To turn the page –
ONE:	'Buried asbestos in
	primary-coloured
	primary school walls.'
TWO:	To pour yourself a Coke or
	a juice or
	a nice-enough Chilean red,
	and to cancel all your half-made plans for
	the rest of the weekend because –
ONE:	This is a good read.
TWO:	To put it down,
	disgusted.
	Embarrased,
	for Em,
	her angst,
	her weakness.
ONE:	To pick it up again.
	To read on.
	To feel it,
	hold it,
	hurl it at the wall to
	see if you can
	make it break,
	her pain,
	Em's pain,

red-raw like open wounds on
public transport and
you just as unwilling to
touch or
look away.

TWO:	Two people.
ONE:	Two people.
TWO:	You, me.
ONE:	Me, you.
BOTH:	Do we –
ONE:	I don't think so.
TWO:	Maybe, we –
ONE:	I don't think so, no.
	Two people,
	you, me and we –
TWO:	Yes?
ONE:	We –
TWO:	What?
ONE:	We size each other up.
TWO:	Do we?
ONE:	Of course we do.
TWO:	It's immediate.
ONE:	Instinctive.
TWO:	Impossible to
	pretend otherwise.
ONE:	It's nothing personal.
TWO:	The opposite of personal.
ONE:	We know the answer
	before we even register we've
	asked the question.
TWO:	Who's bigger.
ONE:	Stronger.
TWO:	Faster.
ONE:	More likely to be volatile.
TWO:	More likely to be versatile.

ONE:	Malleable.
TWO:	Combustible.
ONE:	Who's the dick and
	who's the throat,
	to put it roughly.
TWO:	Crudely.
ONE:	Necessarily.
TWO:	We see,
	we size,
	we fight or
	fuck or
	try to pass
	unnoticed in the night.
BOTH:	You're better than me,
	I know it.
TWO:	In the black of an eye –
ONE:	The bat of a lash –
TWO:	Two shakes of
	a trembling tail –
ONE:	We decide.
	We all do.
TWO:	All the time.
ONE:	Every one of us.
TWO:	Just – a moment.
ONE:	A pulse.
TWO:	Shock.
ONE:	Charge.
TWO:	Charge!
ONE:	Charge!
TWO:	And then it passes.
ONE:	It passes.

TWO:	And we breathe easy.
ONE:	Easier.
	No longer stranded on
	the roofs of
	flooded mouths.
TWO:	But in that moment –
ONE:	We both knew.
TWO:	We both know.
ONE:	Don't we?
TWO:	Don't we?

A second black sack.

This sack,
if there is a sack,
is heavier than the first and
has to be dragged,
slowly and
with great purpose.

If we were on a beach,
a tropical beach,
a tropical island paradise,

(not in a theatre)

then the dragged bag would leave

a great smiling trench in
the pure white sand.

ONE:	Two people.
	Ike and Kay.
TWO:	Kay and Ike.
ONE:	They never quite settled on
	a preferred order in which to
	say their Christian names.
TWO:	Ike is tall with broad shoulders and
	a long, surprisingly thin neck that
	sways above his body.
	Like an eel,
	he thinks,
	on a bad day.
ONE:	On a good day,
	rare good day,
	he focuses on his shoulders and
	doesn't notice the neck
	quite so much.
TWO:	You know this because
	Ike keeps a blog.
ONE:	They both do.
BOTH:	Together.
TWO:	'Ike and Kay's Corner',
	they call it.
	Home decor and
	the occasional
	gratuitously misinformed
	political rant.
ONE:	It's charming, really.
TWO:	All block caps and
	dead links and

	images ripped directly from
	Gwyneth Paltrow's
	goop.com.
ONE:	A solid effort.
TWO:	A happy home.
ONE:	Not the place to wonder
	out loud and
	in public then,
	whether your neck looks like
	a serpent hanging from a
	four-day-old birthday balloon.
TWO:	Not on the blog,
	God no,
	save that for the forums,
	the message boards,
	the dark-desk-drawer-of-the-internet.
ONE:	You know this because you
	Googled Ike's email address,
	after finding it on the
	Ike and Kay's Corner
	'Contact Ike and Kay' page.
TWO:	You were curious.
ONE:	A healthy curiosity.
TWO:	572 posts archived since 2009.
ONE:	You read them all.
	What can you say?
	You're interested in people.
	You're a people-person.
TWO:	You read them all,
	in one long,
	sleepless,

selfless night.

And you know this:

ONE: Ike hates his neck.

TWO: Ike hates his boss.

ONE: Ike dreams alone of
being choked while masturbating but
does not intend to
act on that desire.

TWO: Not yet.

ONE: No, not quite yet.

TWO: And Ike loves Kay.

ONE: 'I love my wife.

I love her more than
all the trees that were ever
chopped down for
reclaimed redwood coffee tables.'

TWO: Kay is tall with
broad shoulders too,
broader even than Ike's,
which is okay,
perfectly okay,
in this open-minded world of
modern dating.

ONE: You know this,
because by now you feel –
invested –
in Ike,
in Kay,
in their happy, happy home and
his three-inch thin neck,
and so you geo-locate the
photo on the homepage of the blog.

TWO:	The X-Pro II filtered photo of
	the two of them outside their house –
ONE:	Green door,
	white shutters –
TWO:	New keys held between
	their two linked hands.
ONE:	'I love her more than eggshell blue,
	more than cocktail glasses sculpted out of
	extinct animal skulls.'
TWO:	You rent a car and
	you leave your house at 4am to
	beat the rush hour.
	It's almost ninety minutes drive but
	like you say,
	you're interested in people.
ONE:	The internet is so impersonal.
TWO:	You want to see them in
	the flesh.
ONE:	'I love her more than intelligent espresso machines,
	more than cowhide lounge chairs with
	the horns still hanging on.'
TWO:	They met at a convention centre.
ONE:	A latter-day love story.
TWO:	You know this because he
	writes about it on the forum on
	somebody else's thread entitled:
	'Structural Integrity of Pre-1940 Roofing'.
ONE:	The moderators give him
	one last warning about
	posting unrelated content.

TWO: She was moving at unusual speed,
         striding across the room towards
         the tea and
         coffee and
         individually-packed biscuit station.
         Didn't even see him until just –

ONE: Before.

TWO: Almost knocked him clean off his feet.

ONE: And Ike's not a small guy,
         clears six foot in dress shoes –

TWO: It is mainly neck, of course.

ONE: 'I love her more than cut-glass and
         razor-sharp edges.
         More than rough-hewn
         bare brick walls
         that leave abrasions
         over exposed skin'.

TWO: They've been in Shepperton going on
         six years now.

ONE: It's beautiful.

TWO: It is beautiful, yes.

ONE: Idyllic, really.

TWO: She takes long walks,
         right across the centre of the fields.

ONE: Ike worries about her safety but
         Kay knows better than to stick to the paths.

TWO: People are
         more dangerous than
         wild animals and
         most people stick to the paths.

ONE:	He's more of a stroll-man,
	Ike is,
	so he'll usually stay at home
	when she walks.
	Do a few bits-and-bobs.
	Work on his projects.
	Internet.
	Live-cam.
	Autoeroticfantasyfiction.com.
	Do-It-Yourself, you know.
TWO:	He's done a beautiful job with the bedroom.
ONE:	As he says on the blog,
	July 1st 2014,
	he can't take all the credit.
	We have Mr Årviksand and
	Madam Blekviva to
	thank for that.
TWO:	He talks about the IKEA like
	they're neighbours.
ONE:	Neighbours?
	Family.
	Really.
	They're a part of our home.
	They live here,
	live here with us,
	with Ike and Kay,
	in this beautiful,
	bountiful,
	well-lit,
	well-stocked,
	Swedish-influenced,

two-storey,

six-window,

one-and-a-half-bedroom and

five-secret-locked-drawers home,

with their internet set to 'incognito' and

both their names below the

personalised letterbox on the

forest green front door.

6.

ONE:	Two people –
TWO:	You, me.
ONE:	Me,
	you.
TWO:	Do we –
ONE:	I don't think so.
TWO:	Maybe, but –
ONE:	I don't think so, no.
TWO:	Maybe at a party or
	a dinner or
	a deserted train station, perhaps?
ONE:	Are you – ?
TWO:	Do you – ?
ONE:	Have we – ?
TWO:	Before – ?
ONE:	Did we – ?
TWO:	Before – ?
ONE:	And we both know.
TWO:	We both exactly know.
ONE:	Who's thinner.
TWO:	Taller.
ONE:	More 'interesting'.
TWO:	Good to be 'interesting'.
ONE:	Good not to blend into a
	blank white wall.
TWO:	Who smells like
	sweat and
	fear and
	insecurity and
	who reeks of
	expensive confidence.

ONE:	Who brushes past in
	Tangiers Mist and
	who lingers like
	last week's wet clothes at the
	bottom of the basket.
TWO:	Who's the dick and
	who's the throat.
ONE:	To put it bluntly.
TWO:	Coarsely.
ONE:	Slam-your-head-into-the-desk-ly.
TWO:	Here till it's just me and
	the cockroaches,
	baby,
	you say through
	half-closed eyes under
	artificial light.
ONE:	Is that a knife between your teeth or
	are you just happy to see me?
TWO:	Is that a knife between your teeth or
	is it just the light reflecting back off mine?
ONE:	But we – ?
TWO:	I don't think so.
ONE:	Maybe we – ?
TWO:	I'm afraid I don't think so, no.
ONE:	Well.
TWO:	It's nice to – ?
ONE:	Yes.
	You too.
TWO:	Pleasure.
ONE:	All mine.

Another bag,
another real-imaginary-pitch-black-sack,
you know the drill, by now.

This one not even a surprise,
except for the feeling.
the eerie feeling,

(smaller than
a single grain of sand lodged
deep in a soft pink throat)

the feeling that maybe,
maybe –
you can hear it breathing?

But you know there's almost certainly no sack, here,
here on the stage,
here in this empty fullness where
'anything is possible', right?

You know there's no sack here, right?

TWO:	Leila you found on the internet, on YouTube. In 2D full colour, trapped in a black plastic box with super-HD capabilities.
ONE:	You've been watching Leila for a while now. Waiting for each new upload in a way that is more masturbatory than you'd publicly admit.
TWO:	Because Leila is hot.
ONE:	Leila is definitely hot.
TWO:	Leila is hot enough that her hotness would unquestionably be consistently referenced by apparently legitimate news sources if she were ever caught up in an international murder trial.
ONE:	You personally contributed 57 of her first 3,118,827 views.
TWO:	57 views of 46 seconds, her with teeth and eyes and tits writ large in front of point-and-shoot camera.

ONE: It's an interesting name, isn't it?
'Point-and-shoot.'

TWO: Leila does make-up tutorials.

ONE: Leila takes requests.

TWO: Leila reads every single comment she receives
and takes the time,
her time,
her precious,
puckered time,
to personally respond.

ONE: Leila is glad you like her four-minute smoky eye.

TWO: Leila is thrilled you shared her frosted lip.

ONE: Leila wants you to update her on your date at
the roller disco.

TWO: Leila hopes your date enjoyed the
Exotic Eye Jewel temporary tattoo she suggested,
she hopes it added an
undefinable air of mystery to your
half hour at the Bombs Away Bowling Lane and
your forty minutes groping in the street outside.

ONE: Leila is not herself a teenager,
but she was one once,
a popular and
provocative one who
moved through the
suburban school system with
previously-unheard-of-ease.

TWO: Leila provides photographic evidence of this,
herself as an untroubled teen,
acne-free and
confident in crop tops.

ONE: Leila wants to use her knowledge,

share her knowledge.

share her recipes for no-bake cakes and

non-alcoholic skinny mojitos,

with all of you,

all of you out there and

insecure, together.

TWO: Leila is happy and

tanned and

perfectly contoured and

she makes you feel –

ONE: Sick.

TWO: She makes you feel –

ONE: Bitter.

TWO: She makes you feel –

better.

Not how she wants to,

intends to,

but better nonetheless.

She makes you feel elite.

She makes you laugh –

at her,

of course,

at her –

and she makes you feel smart.

ONE: She makes you feel anger.

She makes you feel disgust –

TWO: She makes you feel distant,

good-distant,

from the kind of shit she

wallows in and

slathers on

her face.

ONE: She makes you feel –

shit.

TWO: You don't think about it that much.

You don't.

Honestly.

You screenshot it,

it,

her,

sure,

but not enough to

make a folder.

Another folder.

You close your laptop.

You adjust your lights.

You don't go outside because

who does,

these days,

and you go back to

thinking mainly of

yourself.

The thought passes and

you let it pass.

ONE: You don't.

You turn it all back on.

You log back in,

not in your name because

who does,

these days.

You get in touch –

it's good,

of course,
to be in touch.
It's human to reach out,
connect.
You send your words like
darts into
the dark.
Like darts in dark and
just as entertaining.
Leila doesn't take your request to do a
'two black eyes tutorial'.
Leila doesn't respond
to your comment that she should
'step-by-step kill herself'.
Leila doesn't respond to those suggestions or
to any of the 366 others that you post over
a quiet evening,
but in the morning –
Leila has a new video.

TWO: 'I hope that whoever left those messages,
whoever thinks it's funny or
clever to
leave those messages,
those messages,
keels over and
dies alone.
Soon.
Ugly and
alone and
soon.
Because is there

anything
more important
than not dying
ugly and alone?"

ONE: And that's it.
That's all.
And it's funny.
It's funny, right?
And after you scroll through the
rash of messages left by
concerned minors about
how to stave off puffy eyes post-weep,
you lose interest and
roll over to
your junk mail or
your box set or
the next video that will automatically load in the
'Hot Bitch Cries' playlist.
'Is there
anything
more important
than not dying
ugly and alone?"

8

TWO: At this point,
              at this exact moment,
              (although perhaps it's true that maybe
              he has been here all along,
              perhaps it's true that we,
              you,
              any of us,
              just don't notice him earlier,
              don't notice him until it is,
              perhaps,
              in fact,
              perhaps,
              too late),
              at this point,
              a man enters the space.
              A man enters the space and
              the man has a gun.
              Silent and
              present,
              a man with
              a gun.

ONE:	You, me.
	Me, you –
TWO:	And him.
	You, me and
	him.
ONE:	You, me.
	Me, you –
TWO:	And him.
ONE:	Two people –
TWO:	Three people –
ONE:	Two people,
	two people,
	two people –
TWO:	And him.
ONE:	There is no him.
TWO:	There is a him,
	a man,
	there is a man and
	the man has a gun and
	maybe he's always been here.
	Maybe he's always been here,
	watching us.
ONE:	–
TWO:	–
ONE:	Two people.
	You, me –
TWO:	Don't.

ONE:	Right.
	Well.
	Anyway.
	I'm sorry.
	I'm sorry, everybody,
	Because you came here for –
	enjoyment?
	Amusement.
	Distraction.
	And that's not wrong,
	not wrong at all.
	Because you work hard all week and
	the least,
	the very least that
	you deserve
	is distraction.
	You work hard all week and
	you deserve the avoidance of
	discomfort.
	The feeling, that –
	The knowing, that –
	And that was –
	That was –
TWO:	We all know what that was.
ONE:	Nothing.
TWO:	We all know that was –
ONE:	Nothing at all.
	And actually,
	I think we should just
	forget about it,

I think we should all just
forget about it.
Click to a different browser,
different tab,
choose a tab,
any tab –
push it to the
back of our minds behind
the latest celebrity vagina shot and
a looping clip of a middle-aged man being
injured on a miniature trampoline.

TWO: The man with the gun is still there and
not speaking.

ONE: Bury it behind a headline story of
a news anchor accidentally saying the word 'cunt'
and a high-res photo of a dog in
a wig and a bandana.

TWO: The man with the gun has
left his position and is
beginning to
pace.

ONE: Hide it away,
at the furthest reaches of
the deepest freeze,
behind the mini ice-cream sandwiches and
the 14% Assorted Animal Protein Gyoza
Potstickers.

TWO: The man is pacing and
the man has,
as we've said,
the man has a gun,

	in his hands,
	his thick, meaty hands –
ONE:	Throw it from a moving train window,
	like a heroic white man in a VHS B-movie.
	Spray it with bullets like Brad Pitt with
	a cod German accent and a
	this-is-the-real-history-moustache.
TWO:	The man has more guns –
ONE:	Child star.
TWO:	Bigger guns –
ONE:	Shark attack.
TWO:	Faster guns with
	more firepower –
ONE:	Breast implants.
	Butt lift.
TWO:	More attachments –
ONE:	Waxed asshole.
	Bleached asshole.
TWO:	More shiny chrome and
	strings of perfect bullets than
	one man,
	this man,
	this man in
	this room,
	could ever use in six lifetimes.
	More guns than
	any man could
	ever hope or
	fear to
	use.
	And the man,

	the man,
	the man says –
ONE:	'Don't worry.
	Don't worry.
	I'm not here to harm you.
	I don't have a message or
	a threat or
	a ransom note written in
	cut-out letters from the
	Guardian Weekend Style magazine.
	I'm not here for any reason except
	to let you know that – '
TWO:	'I am here.
	I am here.
	And you shouldn't forget about me.
	Won't forget about me.
	I'm a man with a gun.
	I'm six foot four and solid,
	armed and loaded.
	I'm not a metaphor.
	And you should not
	forget about me.'
ONE:	There is no man.
	There is.
	No.
	Man.

11

TWO: The man with the gun is
       still here.

ONE: I don't like this.

TWO: The man with the gun is staring steel-eyed from
       the corner of the room.

ONE: It's not a fucking joke.

TWO: The man with the gun moves
       slowly under
       weight of metal –

ONE: It's not funny,
       if it ever even was.
       You can't just –

TWO: Just –

ONE: Just bring him here.

TWO: He's here.

ONE: He's not.
       He can't be.
       I was here.
       We were here.
       You,
       me,
       everybody was here –

TWO: And now?

ONE: He's here.

TWO: So?

ONE: So?

TWO: It doesn't mean that
       you don't carry on.
       Enjoyment.
       Amusement.

Distraction.
Isn't that what they
always tell us,
always say?
You have to
carry on,
right into
the jaws –

ONE: I can't –

TWO: You have to –

ONE: I don't –

TWO: You don't get to choose to –

ONE: Em.
Em.
Perfectly circular,
Em.

TWO: The man with the gun pauses,
swivels,
all his metal eyes on you.

ONE: Chicken and mushroom pie.
Chicken.
And.
Mushroom.
Pie.
And a Dr. fucking Pepper.
Smiley face with crossed-out eyes.
And Em says that:
'I saw a man, today – '

TWO: The man with the gun
cocks his head.

ONE: 'A man.

Walking towards me at the bus stop,
well-dressed with
a recently-stitched-up-cut
snaking from
raised eyebrow to
cut-glass cheekbone.'

TWO: Like he smells something.
You.
On you.
Don't stop.

ONE: 'Good-looking,
even with the wound.
Especially with
the wound.'

TWO: The man with the gun has
his hand on
his holster.

ONE: 'Like the photos of
soldiers in
Mr Jones' history class,
all neat-parted hair and
clear skin and
jaw and
bone and
never going to
speak to me.
Blown to pieces eighty years ago or
nibbled all apart by rats.
Much better than
the boys I know,
these men who

carried guns and
died.'

TWO: The man with the gun fondles his weapon in
a way that must be
meant to be
intentionally offensive.

ONE: 'Imagining this wounded man,
his stitches bursting and
the blood all
rushing out.
He'd ask me for
a tissue and
it'd start from
there.
I'd tend his wound,
pull out the
stitch and
crawl inside.
He'd let me in to
see beneath.
Imagining insides.
Imagining what's underneath.
Imagining myself fainting,
overcome with
fear or
love or
nausea and
my skull hitting the ground,
splitting open and
upsetting everyone.
True love.

First love.

Chicken and mushroom pie.'

TWO: The man with the gun has
his hand on the gun,
stroking it,
jerking it,
holding its weight and
grinning with pride at it.

ONE: 'Imagining a whole class of
nursery school children gasping.
Maybe they've been on a trip to
the British Museum and
they've seen a real Viking helmet with
real horns that belonged to
something with a real heart and
now they're walking two-by-two and
they see me.
Spilt across the pavement like
a packet of ham.
Hair and
gore and
bits of bone with
stuff stuck to it.
Brains and
blood and
chewing gum.
Him turning away and
not even taking
a piece of
me with
him.

And I'm just frozen to the spot.
Not breathing and
inventing my death through
the eyes of young children.
My disaster at
the hands of
a stranger who'll
have a scar
next year.
And I know,
I know,
that everyone's different,
I know
that we're supposed to
'be yourself',
'you do you',
'this is the new normal',
but still –
that's not really normal.
Is it?'
And here,
actually,
I noticed that her
handwriting changes –
goes wobbly almost,
then suddenly barbed,
peaking like a
TV cardiac arrest,
like she's writing while she's
crying or
maybe just on

public transport.
And then it sort of
smoothes out,
actually sort of smoothes out into
a single line which
runs off the page and
onto the other half of the diary,
onto the space that's usually
designated for the next day's entry.
And that space is empty and
so is the rest of the diary and
the pages are sort of crumpled,
ripped almost,
like maybe there's been
a scuffle or
a confrontation,
a bit like the diary was ripped from her hands
maybe,
on the sticky steep stairs of the 148 maybe,
or perhaps just carried off in a
particularly strong breeze.
And yes,
okay,
maybe that is a drop of blood on
the outside back cover but
people do get nosebleeds,
don't they?
Don't they?

TWO:	The man with the gun –
ONE:	The man with the gun is not moving.
TWO:	The man with the gun is statue-still.
ONE:	The man with the gun is still standing there and still not speaking.
TWO:	And you don't like that, hate that even, stuck like deer in headlights –
ONE:	Searchlights –
TWO:	Sights.
ONE:	He's looking at you. He's looking directly at you. at your shit-eating grin and your greasy eyes and your shaking hands in empty pockets.
TWO:	He's not looking at me.
ONE:	He's looking at you –
TWO:	Me.
ONE:	You.
TWO:	Me.
ONE:	And he is not looking away. He lifts his hand, right hand, and makes a gesture like –
TWO:	'Go on.'
ONE:	He's listening.
TWO:	I know.

ONE: To you.

TWO: I know.

ONE: So tell him.

TWO: What –

ONE: Whatever you know.

Whatever he needs.

Whatever it takes.

Whatever there is,

in you,

in us –

TWO: I don't –

ONE: Just.

Tell.

Him.

TWO: Ike and Kay.

Okay?

But –

no Kay.

No Kay for

one day,

two days,

three days,

four and

each night Ike keeps vigil at

the green front door and

each new dawn he

adds to his

online IKEA wish list.

ONE: Keep going.

TWO: Clicking back and

forth between

the tabs,
eyes staring in
white-socked feet under
artificial light.
Things he thinks she'd like.
Things he wished he'd
bought for her,
back when it was her still here,
not all these boxes.
Not all this stuff.
All these deliveries,
for her,
for not-here her.
Padding like
an animal from
breakfast bar to
empty bed,
small twists of polystyrene,
inedible peanuts,
getting caught
between his toes.
Like walking on
the beach as
a child,
he thinks,
as he adds another
plastic salad spork to his
virtual shopping bag.
He looks for her,
searches for her,
for her name and

finds a lighting company.
Kay Lights.
She always loved light.
'It's one of the things that
makes her special.'
It was one of the first things she told him,
on a smoke break between
conference speakers –
'I love light.
It's just so –
I just love it.'
Ike bought her fairy lights
each Christmas,
every occasion,
strings of them,
reams of them,
whole open armfuls of them,
more and more till
he was sure that they
would one day
set alight and
kill them both.
Sure too that
that was what was
meant to be.
Bodies fused together,
melted together,
wrapped tight in
sixty feet of
LED.

ONE: The man with the gun is
listening,
nodding,
not moving now,
for once.

TWO: I can't –

ONE: Don't stop –

TWO: But how –

ONE: Just don't.
Don't stop.

TWO: He orders the
three-light Quiozel Stargaze floor lamp,
from Kay,
for Kay.
It's beautiful, really.

ONE: It is beautiful, yes.

TWO: Three floating wire cages in
the picture on
the internet,
a little beating filament heart in each.
He used to dream of
being trapped,
caged,
unable to escape.
Of wires,
mesh,
chains.
Now he just dreams of
Kay and
missing.
When it arrives,

the box is six feet tall and
four feet wide.
Like her.
'KAY' in thick black capitals
on every side.
Everywhere you look.
He drags it,
it-her,
it-Kay,
into bed and
under the duvet cover that
she chose.
He sleeps wrapped around it –
sharp cardboard corners
digging into flesh and
leaving marks.
Abrasions.

ONE: The man with the gun is
shifting,
clanking –

TWO: It's not enough.

ONE: He wants more,
needs more –

TWO: Not more –

ONE: Not more –
Just –

TWO: On the fifth day of
the third week of
no Kay and
all these boxes,
all this useless packaging,

Ike wakes to
finds the cardboard,
Kay-cardboard –
on the floor.

ONE: 'I love my wife.'

TWO: Ripped.
Contents upended.
The wire cages
prized apart,
the bulbs inside
each smashed.

ONE: 'I love her more than
shards and
glass and
glowing.'

TWO: Blood in his mouth and
on his bedsheets.
His knuckles.
In the dark of
drawn curtains,
he logs on and
places the order.
Re-order.

ONE: 'I love her more than
one-click purchasing,
more than guaranteed
next-day delivery.'

TWO: He sleeps beside
the fridge
awaiting its
arrival.

	Shadow at the door.
ONE:	Man at the door.
TWO:	Finally.
	Rush to open.
	Sign.
	Collect.
	Caress.
	But next morning,
	finds it smashed again.
	Snakebite of
	a staple under
	ring fingernail.
	Orders again.
ONE:	'More than – '
TWO:	Smashed again.
ONE:	'More than, more than – '
TWO:	A broken hand.
ONE:	Bright purple ring of bruising.
TWO:	Glass embedded far
	beyond his hairline.
ONE:	Shards glistening like
	diamonds in
	his three-inch neck.
TWO:	No wonder she left.
ONE:	Gone.
TWO:	Left.
ONE:	Gone.
TWO:	All alone in
	laptop light with
	bandaged hand,
	he clicks again.

ONE:	Buys again.
TWO:	For Kay.
	For her.
	It's what she'd want.
ONE:	It's what he wants.
TWO:	He doesn't mention
	the cardboard or
	the smashing or
	the missing or
	the broken glass on
	'Ike and Kay's Corner',
	of course he doesn't.
	But it's there.
ONE:	More –
TWO:	In every post about
	embroidered wall hangings,
	every photo essay on
	The Year Of Striking Accent Tones.
ONE:	More –
TWO:	He doesn't miss a day.
	He can't –
	his audience expects.
ONE:	More –
TWO:	He finds himself focusing especially on
	minimalist sculptures made of
	jagged shards and
	twisted metal,
	as the splinters work
	their way into
	his bloodstream.
ONE:	And the man with the gun

clears his throat and smiles –
but still he does not speak.

13.

TWO: The man with the gun is still there,
still fucking there. ONE: You need to speak to him.

TWO: The man with the gun
          cracks his knuckles and
          it sounds like
          a spine.

ONE: You brought him here.

TWO: The man with the gun wears
          bullets like it's no big fucking deal and
          he is still here,
          just like he was before,
          just like he's ever been.

ONE: So –

TWO: So –

ONE: So ask him to leave.

TWO: As if it works like that.
          As if it works a
          thing like that.
          This is –
          beyond.
          This is
          fucking beyond and
          I cannot,
          cannot
          write a
          pleasant fucking post-it note to him to
          'ask him to leave'.
          'Could everyone please,
          please
          remember to

put down the

toilet seat and

turn the lights off

when you leave and

please don't point that

thing

at me because

I'd really feel

much safer

if you didn't.'

ONE: Then give it to him.

TWO: Give what to him?

ONE: Whatever the fuck

he

wants.

TWO: –

ONE: Anything.

Everything.

The truth or

just whatever's left.

TWO: A sound.

A ring.

A flashing mechanical-animal-eye as

your next-gen smartphone winks like

the last one left at

closing time.

ONE: A video.

TWO: Leila.

ONE: Beautiful Leila,

foxy Leila,

you'll-never-guess-what-she-does-with-this-
mascara-Leila and you,
like much of the world,
mortal danger or no,
switch on and
press play.

TWO: The video is just under seven minutes long,
uploaded from somewhere near Acton.

ONE: The man with the gun
clenches his jaw.

TWO: Leila looks straight down the
Creative Live! Cam Chat HD Webcam lens,
right into your eyes and
past them to the
red-raw-back-wall of
your hard skull.

ONE: Tear-stained eyes and
Crest White teeth and
shaking double-Ds.

TWO: Leila weeps and
shivers and
tries hard-but-not-hard-enough
to calm herself as
she tells the world and
us about
her husband.

ONE: Leila has a husband?

TWO: Leila *had* a husband but
that husband is
no longer here,
anymore.

ONE:	The man with the gun
	runs his tongue
	along bared teeth.
TWO:	'It was a normal day.
	How could I know my
	life would change forever.'
ONE:	Leila enjoys a healthy amount of
	dramatic suspense.
TWO:	'When Henry left – '
ONE:	Henry is her husband,
	was her husband,
	which wasn't actually
	explained in the video,
	thank you Leila,
	but was in the
	Daily Mail article that
	MrWhisker313 links to in the
	comments section.
TWO:	'When Henry left –
	how could I know.
	I had no idea.'
ONE:	She emphasises this last part,
	moving closer to
	tearfully eye-fuck the camera.
TWO:	Henry is her husband.
ONE:	Henry was her husband.
TWO:	Henry has disappeared.
ONE:	Henry has,
	as far as you can gather from
	Leila's sighs and fuck-me whispers,
	slipped out the house,

their house,

as Leila slept soundly in

their clean pink bed.

TWO: Slipped out the door and –

ONE: Down the road and –

TWO: Onto a train –

ONE: Then a plane –

TWO: Then a bus across a desert,

then a long walk in ill-fitting boots across

an unforgiving landscape

to pick up weapons he would

forever now call his own.

ONE: He's fighting on the

right side,

of course.

TWO: Of course,

he's fighting on

the right side.

ONE: He's fighting on

whichever side,

whatever side,

the-who-even-fucking-cares-anymore side.

He's fighting on

the side with

more guns,

bigger guns.

more men with

faster guns –

TWO: The man with the gun

spits into his palm,

big gob of

	spit in
	open palm.
ONE:	But still,
	it's not something you
	might have expected from
	a man called Henry –
	and Leila,
	32/f/sad and lonely in West Chiswick,
	is as shocked as any of us.
TWO:	'No idea – '
ONE:	She pauses and
	we collectively hold our breath and
	bite our near-to-bleeding lips.
TWO:	'No idea that that
	was what
	he wanted.'
ONE:	'What he needed.'
TWO:	'What he travelled halfway across
	the whole wide world for,
	to fight in someone else's war for,
	leaving his girlfriend,
	his wife,
	his smoking-hot-and-still-young-still-young-enough-wife,
	leaving her all alone with a webcam and
	an empty house,
	all alone with
	6,000 daily viewers.'
ONE:	'I had no idea.'
TWO:	'But now I do.'
ONE:	'And you do too.'

TWO: 'Because that's really what I wanted to
         share with you,
         with all of you,
         here,
         together,
         the independent women and
         the crop-top teenage girls.'
ONE: 'Don't ever risk your man,
         your love,
         true love,
         the love of
         your true life,
         leaving you.
         Leaving you for
         a fucking desert,
         for fucking Aberjiyan,
         for Kahbullah,
         whatever,
         for scraping and
         blasting and
         bombs from above.'
TWO: 'If that's what he wants – '
ONE: 'What he really, really wants – '
TWO: 'You can give it to him.'
ONE: 'You're a goddess.'
TWO: 'You're an enigma.'
ONE: 'You're a beautiful chameleon.'
TWO: 'Why would he
         even dream of
         leaving,
         when he could have
         exactly what he wants,

	everything he wants,
	right here,
	at home,
	with you?'
ONE:	'The clogged pores.'
TWO:	'The un-exfoliated skin.'
ONE:	'The blood.'
TWO:	'Fresh or dried.'
ONE:	'Both!'
TWO:	'When he could have
	all that,
	at home,
	with you.'
ONE:	'And now – '
TWO:	'I'm going to show you how.'
ONE:	And Leila,
	smiling now with
	bright red eyes,
	like a rabbit,
	like a beautiful,
	terrified,
	chemically-altered rabbit,
	pouting frenziedly into
	the camera,
	shows you what
	she's bought.
TWO:	The prices flash
	across the bottom of
	the screen in
	bright pink
	bubble writing.

ONE:	An animated heart screams 'HAUL!' as Leila blinks and dilates her eyes.
TWO:	A Brillo pad.
ONE:	'Three for a pound!'
TWO:	Sandpaper.
ONE:	'£3.57!'
TWO:	Steel bladed bolt cutters.
ONE:	'Just twenty-seven quid from B&Q!'
TWO:	'A steal!'
ONE:	Garden shears.
TWO:	She calls them 'secateurs', twisted in the word like barbs of wires.
ONE:	'Now, don't be afraid to go the whole Joan of Arc, babes!'
TWO:	'Go the whole Game of Thrones!'
ONE:	'Go the whole prisoner of war, go for it! It's so you, you know it is!'
TWO:	And then – her skin.
ONE:	'Just think of it like high heels – they make you bleed but they look so 'Like' in the photos after.'
TWO:	Sandpaper making tears, abrasions, sun-scorched earth.

ONE: More –

TWO: Blood running down

her sculpted cheek.

ONE: More –

TWO: Tearing out extensions with

bare hands,

hacking at

highlighted hair.

ONE: 'So quick you

can do it in

just minutes!

Don't want to

make him wait

too long!'

TWO: Sharp metal glinting at

her collarbone,

her jawline.

Her eyes.

ONE: Her eyes.

TWO: Keep going.

ONE: Closed now,

screwed up tight,

eyeliner wings long-crashed

into the earth.

TWO: 'Don't forget, define and line, ladies!'

ONE: Her eyebrows almost gone

by now or

just dissolved into

the mess

of her.

TWO: Five minutes and

forty-three seconds.

ONE:	Five minutes.
TWO:	Forty three seconds.
ONE:	The first comment on the video,
	liked 437 times,
	says only:
	'wut…lol.'
TWO:	'Wut.'
ONE:	'Lol.'
TWO:	And when she's done,
	when she pauses,
	when she comes up
	for air with
	a mouthful of dirt,
	of sand,
	half-choking,
	half-caked as
	we all watch,
	when she's done,
	it's done –
ONE:	We hope –
TWO:	It must be done.
ONE:	Then –
TWO:	Then,
	for reasons that are
	hard to understand,
	or reasons that make
	perfect fucking awful sense
	these days,
	these days,
	Leila takes off her shirt,
	with no bra underneath.

	Her skin under there
	not scraped,
	not scuffed,
	of course.
ONE:	You know from movies
	even dead women
	glow.
TWO:	The ones worth watching –
ONE:	They always glow.
TWO:	Thirty seconds pass in silence before,
	for reasons that are
	even harder to understand,
	inexplicable even,
	or absolutely inevitable,
	a man –
ONE:	A man,
	of course,
	a man –
TWO:	Maybe in a ski mask or
	a hockey mask or
	maybe just long-and-black-haired from
	a month in the desert –
ONE:	Bursts into the shot behind her –
TWO:	Covering her eyes –
ONE:	Covering her breasts –
TWO:	Covering her mouth –
ONE:	Covering the camera –
TWO:	And in the darkness,
	in the muffled darkness of
	human skin on
	manufactured lens,

	in the empty space in which
	your brain leans forward
	half-expecting to hear the word:
BOTH:	'Cut' –
TWO:	We hear a different sound.
ONE:	A sound like this –
TWO:	No, more like this –
ONE:	Maybe this –
TWO:	Like this –
ONE:	Like this –
TWO:	Like this –
ONE:	Like this –
TWO:	Like this –
ONE:	Like this –
TWO:	Like this –
ONE:	Like this –
TWO:	Like that but longer,
	harsher,
	more terrifying,
	more absolute,
	more like the
	absolute-end-of-the-fucking-world
	as we know or
	could ever imagine it and
	the sound,
	the sound,
	the fucking sound,
	suction-tubes itself to
	the inside of your skull and
	stays put well after,
	well,

well,
well after the
video feed eventually ends.

There is a long silence now.

A long silence and
we sit in hard seats with
harder thoughts,
of guns and
violence and
cold hands in
strange places and
combustible appliances that
we fear we may have
left plugged in as
we travelled
far, far away from home.

A long silence,

punctuated by
the sound of pacing,
heavy boots and metal.

And then,
the pacing stops.

This section of the text has been rendered unreadable by bullet holes.

ONE:	Me, you.
TWO:	You, me.
ONE:	Please.
TWO:	No.
ONE:	Please, no.
	We need –
TWO:	More.
ONE:	Not more –
TWO:	Not more –
ONE:	No more.
	I can't.
	Not anymore,
	no more –
	I can't.
	I want to go.
	Go back.
TWO:	To where?
ONE:	Before.
TWO:	You can't.
	We can't.
ONE:	I want to go back to
	the long before.
	To where the dark is
	just the dark and
	guns are only
	cartoon-silhouettes of guns.
	To childhood –
	to riding our bikes fast down
	steep hills with no helmets.
	To bones that bounce,

not break.
To sleep that comes and
trees still thick enough
with leaves to
hide the razor wire in
the fields beyond.
To no strangers shivering in
the corner of the room and
we don't fear to
look each other in the eye
at night time.
To no gunman.

TWO: No terrified hostages.

ONE: Somewhere in the world, maybe –

TWO: Somewhere in the world, sure –

ONE: But not here.

TWO: Not here and
not tonight.

ONE: Go back to heroes.
Some villains,
sure,
some –
but mainly heroes,
overwhelmingly,
impossibly heroes,
in the end at least.
Good guys.
Leather coats and
bullet-proof narratives.
To trust.

TWO: Trust.

ONE:	Companionship.
TWO:	Com-pan-ion-ship.
ONE:	Generosity.
TWO:	Kindness.
ONE:	Truth.
TWO:	The human spirit.
ONE:	The comfort
	of knowing that you are
	not alone and
	that this world is
	built on constancy.
TWO:	That this world is not,
	indeed,
	random.
ONE:	Death does not lurk in
	darkened corners or
	behind each shaded motorcycle visor.
TWO:	Disaster is not
	around the corner or
	on the tip of
	every sharpened tongue.
ONE:	You will not die today.
TWO:	You will not need to feel ashamed.
ONE:	You will not be
	abandoned by loved ones or
	smirked at in the street by
	aesthetically-intimidating strangers.
TWO:	You will not need to imagine
	impending death through
	the averted eyes of tourists.
	When you return,
	to your home –

ONE:	This home –
TWO:	This home of you and
	the people and
	belongings and
	technology you love –
ONE:	You deserve to know that
	it will be exactly as you left it.
TWO:	The walls still carefully arranged with
	photographs of friends and family,
	captured in a constant state of
	smiling affirmation.
ONE:	You are good.
TWO:	You are right.
ONE:	You are safe.
TWO:	And we are here with you.
ONE:	We are happy and
	attractive and
	we smile without
	ever not meaning it and
	we are your close friend,
	your invaluable family member,
	here with you,
	always,
	here with Em and
	Ike and
	Kay and
	Leila,
	Henry even,
	the scar-faced man,
	MrWhisker313,
	Mr Årviksand and

Madam Blekviva and

your fleet of identical sons all named Billy,

walking hand-in-hand,

together.

TWO: We are here with you,

constantly.

ONE: You, me,

TWO: Me, you.

ONE: We are here with you,

always.

TWO: And we are –

sorry.

ONE: We are sorry.

TWO: Gather the children

tight at night and

tell them stories

about how

we are sorry.

ONE: When there are

no more stories then

just tell them truth.

TWO: Truth or

whatever we

still have.

ONE: Tell them about trust and

luck and

safety and

coincidence.

TWO: About propaganda and

probability.

ONE: About the likelihood –

TWO:	The increasing likelihood –
ONE:	The seemingly,
	feeling-ly,
	increasing likelihood
	that it will be –
TWO:	You.
ONE:	You.
TWO:	Me.
	You.
ONE:	Yours.
TWO:	Your home the one
	with the broken windows.
ONE:	Your door the one
	with the blown-off hinge.
TWO:	Your chin the one that
	cracks like concrete in a quake and
	your body –
ONE:	Your body the one with
	real fear and
	hot blood and
	urine.
TWO:	–
ONE:	It's not a game.
TWO:	I know.
ONE:	It's not funny anymore.
TWO:	I don't think that
	it ever was.
ONE:	I didn't want this.
TWO:	I don't think
	any of us did.
ONE:	I want to go back.

TWO:	I'm afraid.
ONE:	Don't say that.
TWO:	I'm afraid we
	can only go forward.

15.

ONE: All the things we are.

TWO: All the things we could have become.

ONE: We need more – time.

TWO: Not more –

Not more –

Just –

ONE: More time.

TWO: Yes, more – time.

ONE: Everything would have been better.

TWO: We would have been better.

ONE: We would have made amends.

TWO: We would have earned forgiveness.

ONE: We would have –

TWO: Started over and –

ONE: We would have been –

much better.

TWO: So –

ONE: So –

TWO: Much better.

ONE: If we only had more – time.

TWO: Everybody is here.

ONE: Everybody is here,

together.

TWO: Em with pen stains and

dried blood on her nostrils.

ONE: Ike with snake neck and

empty search history.

TWO: Leila, shivering now with

no shirt still.

ONE: She has a shirt.

Please.

I'm so sick –

TWO: She doesn't have a shirt.

She doesn't get a shirt.

We know from movies,

from history,

from him –

she doesn't get a shirt.

ONE: Everybody is here –

TWO: Everybody is here,

together.

ONE: Why?

TWO: Because we brought them here,

because we,

you,

I,

brought them here.

ONE: Why?

TWO: It was necessary.

ONE: How?

TWO: It was justified.

It was funny.

It was stupid.

It was a way to

pass the time.

It wasn't worth

dying for,

but what is?

ONE: These days.

TWO: What is?

ONE: Why them?

TWO:	Because it had to be
	somebody.
	Because we wanted them.
	We needed them,
	we found them,
	sought them out and
	brought them here,
	together.
	And maybe you would call that violence or
	maybe you would call it
	good old-fashioned entertainment.
ONE:	Maybe we need women to be murdered so we can
	put their pretty pictures in the paper.
TWO:	Maybe we need children to
	go missing so we can
	remember to hug ours tight as
	we tuck them into tiny beds.
ONE:	Maybe we need our neighbours' houses to
	spontaneously combust on fire so
	we know what we would
	save from the burning rubble when
	the morning comes and
	we need other people to be
	tortured,
	kidnapped,
	robbed at knife point and
	strung up by their ankles,
	right here or
	on the other side of the world,
	outside your window or
	in the confines of your TV screen,

	so that we can be
	relieved that
	they aren't us.
TWO:	Everybody is here.
ONE:	The man is here.
	The man is watching.
TWO:	Everyone is watching.
ONE:	Everyone is kneeling.
	Everyone is kneeling,
	with blindfolds and
	cable ties and
	whispered pleas for forgiveness,
	just like how
	you've seen it on TV.
TWO:	And now,
	now the camera pans 360,
	up and over and
	now we zoom in deep beyond
	the skin and
	flesh and
	3D-rendered
	bright red blood vessels.
ONE:	And now –
	Leila dissolves in
	an HD explosion of teeth and
	tits and
	perfectly-curled-whilst-crying eyelashes.
TWO:	And now –
	Ike is nailed,
	biblically,
	to the door of his

	forest-green-themed starter home with
	a matching pair of cast-iron L-brackets.
ONE:	And Em just keeps imagining
	her death in 3D forever,
	through the eyes of
	ambivalent children and
	attractive strangers.
TWO:	The man with the gun is
	still here.
	Waiting –
ONE:	For –
TWO:	For –
ONE:	So, maybe –
	Ike isn't nailed.
	Crucified yes,
	but not with nails.
	Not metal –
	plastic.
	Coloured plastic in
	artificial-sugar shades.
	Saccharine plastic in
	the shape of
	dog anuses,
	the IKEA Bästis range,
	for just £1 a piece,
	in the bargain bin for
	chump-fucking-change.
TWO:	He's still –
ONE:	He's still here.
TWO:	I can't –
	there's nothing more –

ONE:	There must –
	there has to be –
TWO:	So maybe then –
	Em dies.
	Actually dies.
	Em dies alone and
	then,
	then –
	is born again,
	to watch her death
	on 24-hour repeat,
	on a dedicated satellite channel,
	with the same fucking ads in between
	each episode,
	over and
	over and
	over and
	over again.
	Jingling ads for
	annual insurance against
	hurricanes,
	car crashes,
	inevitable car crashes,
	good money bet on
	loss and
	hurt and
	death and
	violence –
ONE:	What does he –
TWO:	What do we –
ONE:	I'm frightened.

TWO:	Don't say that.
	Don't fucking ever say that.
	Say anything but that.
	Say anything.
ONE:	So maybe –
	Leila doesn't explode.
	Maybe that's too fast,
	too generous.
	Maybe she's torn in two,
	in three,
	four,
	five.
	Maybe we take out her
	£6000 cosmetic dental veneers,
	one by one,
	with a wrench or
	a spanner or
	any of the
	heavy,
	rusted,
	metal tools that we
	don't remember the
	names of now,
	if we ever,
	if we ever even did.
	Pull each one out and
	lay them neat in rows.
	The edges of them stained a
	sugar-almond pink,
	that's how you know that
	it's a girl.

Vomit if you have to then
right back to it.
Thirty-two teeth,
thirty-two teeth in all,
lined up like
tiny toy soldiers,
these made-up artificial teeth.
One tooth still shining with
a Crystal Clear
2.3mm
stick-on Swarovski crystal tooth gem,
in Ruby Bright for
that perfect flash of
after-dinner wonder –

TWO: Don't –
ONE: What –
TWO: It won't –
ONE: What –
TWO: Stop.
ONE: What –
TWO: Him.
It.
All of it.
It's not enough and
it won't ever be
enough.
It'll come.
It'll come,
whatever it is,
for all of us.
Look at it.

At them.
At us and
what we've made.
Him, there.
What we've done and
what we know
we'll do again.

ONE: There wasn't ever
any other way.
We've always been before
the now,
this now.
No more before –
it's here.

TWO: There's nothing more to say –

ONE: Nothing more that
you can think
to say –

TWO: No more nosebleeds.

ONE: No more screaming women.

TWO: No more men with secrets and
bruised knuckles.

ONE: No more body parts in
acid baths.

TWO: No more cold stone slabs.

ONE: No more high-definition disembowelments.

TWO: No more edited beheadings.

ONE: No more cut-out tongues and
scooped-out eyeballs.

TWO: No more talk of
this or

	that or
	them because
	it's here.
ONE:	No more imagining.
TWO:	No more conjuring.
ONE:	No more need to
	scare yourself because
	it's here.
TWO:	It's here.
ONE:	It's here.
TWO:	It's here.
ONE:	He's here.
TWO:	I'm sorry.
ONE:	Look at him.
TWO:	Look at him.

16

ONE: And now,

finally,

fucking finally,

finally,

please,

now –

the man with the gun speaks,

now that everyone is here together.

TWO: Now that everybody sees that

he is here,

we are here,

together.

ONE: Now that there is

no more –

TWO: No more –

ONE: No more 'just – before'.

TWO: The man with the gun speaks and

when he speaks we listen.

ONE: The man with the gun speaks and

none of us speak over him.

TWO: The man with the gun speaks

about threat and

about violence.

ONE: About trust and

terror and

explosives left in

public bathrooms.

TWO: About false flags,

false alarms,

phantom limbs.

ONE: About a real magazine called
        Girls and Corpses and
        about Craigslist killers and
        cannibal chat rooms and
        about how, really,
        it's a broken-fucking-fucking-broken world when we
        need to specify which
        internet-famous-cannibal-fantasist we're referring to.

TWO: The man with the gun stands silhouetted,
        back-lit against your brain.

ONE: The man with the gun stands and
        from this angle,
        he looks smaller than
        he did from
        far away.

TWO: The man with the gun stands and
        his eyeline meets yours,
        no longer towering.

ONE: He stands stock still and
        his outline looks like a
        silhouette-anyone.

TWO: He stands and
        in his hands,
        you see it there.

ONE: Finally.

TWO: Just like you knew it would be.

ONE: He holds it up to you,
        out to you,
        laid prone across his
        open arms like
        a Christmas present or
        a child pulled from water.

TWO:	You wonder if it would be
	cold to touch or
	maybe warm and
	which would be the worse.
ONE:	He holds it up and
	in this light it
	looks itself alive.
TWO:	Moving parts.
ONE:	Body parts.
TWO:	Steel and
	aluminium.
ONE:	Copper,
	tin and
	zinc.
TWO:	Wood.
	Minerals.
	Clay.
	Dirt.
	Trees.
ONE:	Iron,
	turning rock-face red beneath your feet.
	Mountains and
	the things you'll find inside.
TWO:	Tiny veins or
	bones,
	small knuckled worth
	that was dug up,
	chopped down or
	squeezed and
	heated till –
ONE:	Until.

TWO:	All begun as natural and
	then becomes –
ONE:	This.
TWO:	This.
ONE:	This beast.
TWO:	The man with the gun opens his mouth and
	a tiny teardrop of saliva leaps beyond,
	landing in the space between your feet.
	Near enough,
	terribly near enough,
	to touch.
ONE:	You feel your own mouth,
	parched,
	but some there too.
TWO:	The same.
ONE:	But different.
TWO:	But the same, still.
ONE:	The man with the gun speaks and
	his voice sounds faint and
	far away,
	like an old man or
	like your mother on
	a telephone.
TWO:	He speaks and
	he sounds like
	a neighbour you
	once had as
	a child,
	like the primary school teacher
	who taught you numbers and
	straight lines.

ONE:	He speaks and
	he says –
TWO:	You.
ONE:	Me.
TWO:	Me.
ONE:	You.
TWO:	Do we –
ONE:	I don't think so.
TWO:	Maybe, we –
ONE:	I don't think so, no.
TWO:	Two people,
	you,
	me and
	we are –
ONE:	Not so –
TWO:	Not so –
BOTH:	Different.
ONE:	Not so.
TWO:	Not so.
ONE:	The man has a gun and
	the man is a woman,
	swollen by pregnancy or
	maybe just starvation,
	staring you down with
	hot gun on tight belly,
	as you roar past on
	sixteen rubber wheels.
TWO:	The man has a gun and
	the man is a soldier,
	far from home with
	no-words-but-no-longer-wonder at

the size and
scale of trouble
in this too-big world.

ONE: The man has a gun and
the man is a father and
he doesn't have the time,
the great privilege of time,
of meaning,
to make you understand,
he just
needs this,
through gritted teeth,
needs to do this and
he's sorry,
sure,
but he doesn't have the time or
language,
to say even that.

TWO: The man has a gun and
the man is a child,
a tiny child,
dirty-faced with thin limbs and
bombed-out-brain and
eyes like you've only ever seen at
the animal shelter.

ONE: And the child says, yes.
That's what you think.
Animals.
All of us.

TWO: You think of us as animals and
the best that you can hope for is that

we're caged not loose.
Don't dare to let us
wander free,
in your mind or
otherwise.

ONE: The man has a gun and
the man looks
just like –
you.

TWO: Like –
you.

ONE: Like any of us,
all of us –
you.

TWO: Like the shadow in the
politely frightened
space between
your neighbor and
your shoulder.

ONE: Like the shadow in the
hole beneath your eyes.

TWO: Like the shape of a coat,
scrunched and creeping
underneath a hard-backed seat.

ONE: Like a dropped ID card,
in the scrum for
the exit or
the bar.

TWO: Like the darkness
in between each and
everyone of us and

just like what
we each don't see
when we finally
turn our backs
to leave.

They turn and look at him.
Lights up.

By the same author

In the Night Time (Before the Sun Rises)
A baby cries. A bottle breaks. A window smashes. Over the course of one night, mum and dad try to still their screaming infant – but as the hours grow longer, the world becomes elastic around them, and the horrors that scar our planet crash in to the baby's room. Should they ever have brought this child into such a wounded world?
9781783193134

WWW.OBERONBOOKS.COM

Follow us on www.twitter.com/@oberonbooks
& www.facebook.com/OberonBooksLondon